D0939134

LinkedIn Marketing in 2019 Made (Stupidly) Easy

Vol.6 of the "Small Business Marketing Made (Stupidly) Easy" Collection

by Michael Clarke

Founder, Punk Rock Marketing

Published in USA by: Punk Rock Marketing

Michael Clarke

© Copyright 2018

ISBN-13: 978-1-970119-15-2

ISBN-10: 1-970119-15-2

Table of Contents

Chapter 5: Blatant Profiteer's Guide to Creating (and Running) LinkedIn Groups 82

Chapter 6: How to Use LinkedIn Pulse for Complete (and Total) World Domination.......106

Chapter 7: Your Super-Quick Guide to LinkedIn Ads That Don't Suck 121

About the Author

Michael Clarke is a former cubicle monkey turned social media marketing consultant and author.

He is also the owner of the world's most neurotic Jack Russell Terrier.

Also By Michael Clarke

TWITTER MARKETING IN 2019 MADE
(STUPIDLY) EASY

VIDEO MARKETING IN 2019 MADE
STUPIDLY EASY

FACEBOOK MARKETING IN 2019 MADE
STUPIDLY EASY

PINTEREST MARKETING IN 2019 MADE
STUPIDLY EASY

INSTAGRAM MARKETING IN 2019 MADE
STUPIDLY EASY

EMAIL MARKETING IN 2019 MADE
STUPIDLY EASY

SEARCH ENGINE OPTIMIZATION IN
2019 MADE STUPIDLY EASY

A Special FREE Gift for You!

If you'd like FREE instant access to my seminar "How to Make a Damn Good Living With Social Media (Even If You Hate Social Media" then head over to **PunkRockMarketing.com/Free**. (What else you gonna do? Watch another "Twilight" movie?!)

Prologue: Why LinkedIn Might Be the Most Amazing Marketing Tool (You're Not Using)

I shouldn't be writing this book.

I should probably keep my LinkedIn marketing insights to myself.

I should probably tell you to REFUND this book and get your money back because:

- LinkedIn won't work for your type of business (Especially if you don't play in the B2B (business-to-business) space)
- LinkedIn ad costs are ultra-expensive

(Minimum of $2/click)

- LinkedIn sends out more spammy email notifications than ProFlowers (and I didn't think that was possible)

So, there's nothing for you to see here. LinkedIn marketing won't do much for your business and I'm sorry to have wasted your time.

Except…

…LinkedIn might possibly be my favorite method for lead-generation for a few, kick-ass marketing reasons:

- **People who visit LinkedIn are "ready" to do business.** This is not a social networking site filled with cat meme pictures and videos of a Trump presidential rally. This is a social platform about making connections — and furthering one's career.
- **The average household income for LinkedIn users is 109K per year.** MUCH larger than any other social network.

- **LinkedIn is a perfect place to contact, not just future customers, but future partners.** Even if the only people who buy your products are sixteen-year-old shut-ins who play "World of Warcraft" all day, LinkedIn is perfect for connecting with strategic partners who can help move the needle on your business.

- **LinkedIn Groups (I predict) will become the new email list.** Creating, owning and running a LinkedIn Group will soon be more profitable than conventional email lists 10x as big.

- **LinkedIn is mega-respected by the Googlebots.** Meaning a tricked-out LinkedIn Company profile is not only good for your branding, it's vital for your SEO.

- **LinkedIn provides me and my clients the biggest ROI in terms of marketing time, and money spent.** The more ads we buy and LinkedIn emails we write, the more money we make. It's that simple.

And in this humble tome you're holding (or listening to) I will walk you through each of these methods every step of the way. (And show you my favorite, no-brainer lead generation technique…no matter what you're trying to sell.)

But you're probably not interested in any of that. You're probably just fine marketing things the way you are currently. And if so, awesome. I wish you much luck. (And I'll look for you on "Shark Tank.")

But if you'd like to learn how to use LinkedIn Marketing in some powerful (if slightly sneaky) ways, then I encourage you to keep reading.

All I ask is you take the solemn oath of the "League of Inner Circle LinkedIn Marketing Ninjas…"

And that is by holding up your right hand (or left, we're not picky) and solemnly declare:

"I hereby promise to use my newfound LinkedIn Marketing skills for good and not for evil. (And by evil we mean selling more of those "Big

Mouth Billy Bass" singing wall hangings.)"

So, if you're ready to proceed, in a non-Billy Bass world, let's begin by creating you the most kick-ass, awesome LinkedIn Profile that ever existed.

Chapter 1:

5 Steps to a Kick-Ass LinkedIn Marketing Funnel

"Perfection is achieved not when there is nothing more to add, but when there is nothing left to take away."

-Antoine De Saint-Exupery

Before we jump into the nitty-gritty of LinkedIn marketing — and cover the ins and outs of LinkedIn groups and that oddly named "LinkedIn Pulse" — there are a few things we gotta have in place to make sure your LinkedIn efforts actually make you money…

…and not just "pad" your LinkedIn follower

count.

Many of these steps you might already have checked off your marketing to-do list. But if it's been awhile since you looked at these pillars of your business, I encourage you to give each of these a software upgrade.

Leads generated on LinkedIn can be some of the most valuable contacts you make in your business. (But having your marketing funnel set up beforehand will save you not only time — but a crap load of money.)

So here are my 5 Steps to Developing a Kick-Ass LinkedIn Marketing Funnel:

Kick-Ass LinkedIn Marketing Funnel Step #1: Create A Bite-Sized Freebie Thing-a-Ma-Jiggy (That's Easy to Consume)

I know we'd all LOVE to post links to our sales page on LinkedIn and sit on a beach in Aruba sipping $18 drinks with umbrellas in them as we count our profits.

But that's not quite how marketing on LinkedIn works. Instead, the process works something like this:

1. Turn strangers into connections
2. Turn connections into email subscribers/partners/media contacts
3. Turn subscribers into customers
4. Leverage customers/partners/media contacts to promote our business on LinkedIn
5. Rinse and repeat

Now we're gonna cover each of these in more detail as we go, but for now know if I could give you just one LinkedIn ninja-marketing hack it would be this…

…offer folks an INCENTIVE to be added to your network of connections.

I know you feel your dazzling wit — and

immense job experience — is an instant draw to any would-be LinkedIn connection…

…but people NEED more convincing. (Especially since they fear a torrent of spammy LinkedIn emails if they accept your invitation.)

However, if you offer something SMALL and FREE to would-be LinkedIn connections, then you'll separate yourself from the rest of the LinkedIn marketing pack.

Now this FREE THING doesn't have to be BIG or comprehensive. Just a bite-sized (but juicy) tip that helps your ideal customer with one of their biggest, annoying obstacles. (And which lays the groundwork for them to opt-in to your email list.)

Which is why you'll need…

Kick-Ass LinkedIn Marketing Funnel Step #2: Create a Slightly More Expansive Freebie Thing-a-majiggy (That Converts)

Now this FREEBIE is more comprehensive than the freebie in Step #1. (As it should be, you are asking for more of a commitment here — such as an email address or phone number or both.)

And the FREEBIE can take the form of things like:

- Case studies
- Insider guides
- Cheat Sheets
- Webinars
- Seminar
- Special reports
- Resource guide

What works best is if this FREEBIE builds on the topic presented in your earlier freebie.

For instance, with one of my clients who works in the network security space, his "mini-freebie" is: "My #1 secret to safeguarding your business from DNS attacks from abroad (and it takes 5 minutes to set up.)"

This one is a great (bite-sized) tip that crushes it for gathering connections from CTO (Chief Technical Officers) with companies of all sizes.

And then his "larger freebie" is a (recorded) webinar in which he walks prospects through the "5 Biggest Mistakes CTOs Make When Choosing a Network Security Solution."

But both are connected to each other. (And "feel" to the consumer like one extended conversation.)

Now NOT every single new connection you get will opt in for your BIGGER freebie. But we usually get a 50-60% opt-in rate for new connections.

And considering our "connection rate" is most likely to be up 50%, because of our mini-freebie, this is found money.

Kick-Ass LinkedIn Marketing Funnel Step #3: Set Up a Way to Collect Email Addresses

You most likely already have this in place. So I won't belabor the point.

But you'll need two things in place to make your "larger freebie" translate into future profits. And that is:

- **A Landing Page** (Where prospects provide their email and/or phone number)
- **An email autoresponder** (That collects the contact info and then delivers the FREEBIE)

I use LeadPages (for my landing page duties) and ConvertKit (for my email stuff). Both are affordable and make my business appear way more professional and organized than it is.

But you can use any number of companies who offer that service. Just make sure your landing page is as simple as can be and that means:

- A picture of your freebie
- A place to collect contact info
- Headline copy that lets people know what they're gonna get

Kick-Ass LinkedIn Marketing Funnel Step #4: 2-3 Follow Up Emails (That Tell Stories)

This is where most folks' LinkedIn marketing efforts fall short. (Well, that, and their constant need to fill their profile with "certifications" nobody has ever heard of.)

When somebody FIRST opts in to your email list they are both at their most skeptical — "Who is this guy and why does he want to keep emailing me?" — and they're most likely to buy something from you.

They do after all have a problem/concern they need help with. And they want it solved…YESTERDAY!

The key is to write an email follow-up sequence for new opt-ins (I like to send 2-3 over that first week) that tells stories (and subtly sells.)

Forget overt sales pitches and "Grab your 50% off coupon" missives. They don't work anymore.

Instead tell "stories" about you — or your customers — and how they overcame their challenges. (And don't sell until email #3.)

If you're unsure how to do this, just follow this oldie-but-goodie formula:

- **Email #1** - Problem (Touch on the biggest problem your leads are facing, hint at solution)
- **Email #2** - Agitate (Make the problem emotional, urgent)
- **Email #3** - Solve (Offer 'em the solution — which is your product)

At the risk of being a shill, I wrote an entire book on the subject — "Email Marketing Made (Stupidly) Easy" — so check it out if you need a more thorough walk-through.

But if you need the "Cliffs Notes" version, write three emails — following that problem/agitate/solve — and you'll stand out from the rest of the LinkedIn marketing pack.

Kick-Ass LinkedIn Marketing Funnel Step #5: Take a Tour of Your Marketing Funnel

So, this is a tip I got from a super-expensive, otherwise-worthless Mastermind seminar — trust me I'd rather have the Home Theater system I could have bought with the 10K — in which one member mentioned every three months he "plays" prospect and goes through every aspect of his marketing funnel, as if he were a customer.

And whether you follow the stringent 3-month

directive, I recommend before you plunge headlong into the deep end of the LinkedIn marketing pool, you go through your own marketing funnel. (Or have a critical friend or family member do it for you.)

- Does the sales copy adequately speak to the needs of your new leads/subscribers?
- Are you missing any opportunities for upsells — or down sells — or affiliate income that could boost your bottom line?
- Is there a disconnect, at any point, between the message you're trying to send out (and the market you're hoping will receive it)?

Doing this alone will boost your conversion rates, each step of the way, at least 15%. (Which will put enough money in the bank for you to buy those home theater speakers you've had your eye on.)

Chapter One Key Takeaways:

- **Having your LinkedIn marketing funnel set up beforehand will save you time** (and make you more money.) The author wishes he had done this. God, how he wishes he had done this.

- **Once someone has become a "connection," you'll want to move them over to a subscriber.** And for that you'll want a more comprehensive, detailed freebie. (Special reports, resource guides, and cheat sheets work great for this.)

- **Most likely you'll already have this, but you'll need a landing page that collects email addresses** (I use LeadPages) and an email autoresponder to send out automated email messages and deliver your freebie. (I use ConvertKit.) But you can use whatever you like.

- **One of the most neglected parts of a**

LinkedIn marketing plan is the follow-up emails.** I recommend three emails (spaced out over a couple of days) that follow the tried-and-true formula of Problem/Agitate/Solution. (And then in the third email you link up the solution to YOUR product.)

- **The final STEP to a kick-ass LinkedIn marketing funnel is a quick (though highly effective) tour of your marketing funnel** — from start to finish. You could either do it yourself, or have somebody else do it, but checking every element for any weird messaging or unclear benefits will make you money down the line. (Oh, I wish I had done that earlier.)

Chapter 2:

How to Create a LinkedIn Profile That Doesn't Suck

"Nothing succeeds like the appearance of success."
-Christopher Lasch

Even the most novice of LinkedIn users knows it's a platform which is a) business-focused and b) is all about the power of an individual's profile.

That's because a LinkedIn profile isn't just a collection of vital statistics. It's a:

- Virtual resume
- Lead-generation tool
- High-profile Google search result

- Company billboard
- Future employee recruiter
- Fantastic place to showcase any piece of content that you or your team creates

Unfortunately, having a LinkedIn profile that's incomplete, or complete with the WRONG self-serving info — or a profile as boring as a Downton Abbey marathon — will not hurt your chances to gain new business. (But act as a 24-hour repellent for any future LinkedIn marketing activity.)

So, here's my 7-Step LinkedIn Profile Awesomeness Checklist:

(Note: I'm gonna assume you already have a LinkedIn profile created. If not, head over to LinkedIn.com/start/join and create one. It's dead-easy, and they make it simple to find new contacts through your email address.)

LinkedIn Profile Awesomeness Step #1: Create a Marketing-Friendly Public Profile URL

Your LinkedIn public profile URL is the web address where people can find all your LinkedIn goodness. (Example: Linkedin.com/li/PublicProfileURL.)

But what most people don't know is they can change this Public Profile URL anytime they want, up to five times every 180 days.

Not like Facebook, which requires you enlist your firstborn into indentured servitude to change your Fan Page username.

Now you don't want to change your URL as often as Taylor Swift changes boyfriends.

But if you don't quite have your LinkedIn marketing presence built out just yet, or you find your public profile URL as boring as a C-SPAN congressional vote, then think about including one of the following in your public profile URL:

- **The name of your business**
  (LinkedIn.com/BillsHouseofPotpourri)
- **Your name accompanied by occupation**
  (LinkedIn.com/MattJonesDenverRealtor)
- **Keyword-based URL**
  (LinkedIn.com/BestPortlandPizza)

You want to balance common-sense discoverability — what would look good on a business card? — with search-engine keyword considerations. (Your LinkedIn public profile URL will by and large determine your profile's Google popularity.)

LinkedIn Profile Awesomeness Step #2: Upload a LinkedIn Photo That Doesn't Suck

I'm sure you already know this, but you need a good, professional photo to make an impression on LinkedIn. (And dim, shaky, out-of-focus smart phone selfies won't cut it.)

Now I'm not a pro photographer (by any stretch) but I can tell you:

- **Outdoor photos — and well-lit interiors — are the best way to go.** No quick pics taken in the hallway of your neon-lit office hallway.

- **Mornings and early evenings are the best times to take outdoor photos.** The light is best then.

- **Always try to keep the light behind the camera, facing the subject.** Light pointing directly into the camera will make you look like a zombie.

- **Find a talented (and under-employed) photographer on Craigslist to help you out.** Especially if nobody on your team can help you out. They're cheap, and most of the time you'll get great results.

LinkedIn Profile Awesomeness Step #3: Upload a LinkedIn Background Photo of Your Team (or Customers) That Doesn't Suck

Again, I am NOT in the graphic-design caste, so I can't give you a ton of "creative" suggestions for your LinkedIn background photo.

But here's what I've learned so far:

- **The ideal size for these background photos is 1400 x 425 pixels.** And they mean it! Anything not in that ratio will look awful.

- **Pictures of people, including you, work best.** Super-large logos and bit call-to-actions come as spammy and annoying.

- **You — or your customers — working directly with your products or services work best.** Give people a snapshot of the inner-workings of your business. (Worth 1000 words of sales copy.)

- **If you don't have a product, just set up a "faux" speaking event.** Fill a conference room with employees, or random strangers, and take a picture of you "working." (It'll be way better than a logo.)

LinkedIn Profile Awesomeness Step #4: Use Your "Name" Field Like a Total Marketing Ninja

This might be my most favorite (though sneaky) trick in this whole profile bunch. And that is use your "name" field to maximum marketing exposure by including both your "name" and "occupation."

So it would look something like this: "Tom Brady - New England Patriots QB - Professional Uggs Model."

Why would we want to do this? Don't we specify our occupation in the "Professional Headline" section?

A couple of important reasons we want to do things this way:

- **Your "name" field is one of the biggest SEO on-page factors for your LinkedIn Profile**. Why not get in any occupational or business keywords in there to help you get found in the LinkedIn Search bar?
- **It helps your profile stand out**. Hardly anybody does this.
- **We're gonna use the "professional headline" section** to an even more devious marketing end.

Speaking of devious marketing…

LinkedIn Profile Awesomeness Step #5: Ask a Question in Your Professional Headline

I can tell you, without exaggeration, this one technique alone has helped me and my clients boost our LinkedIn marketing lead acquisition by 200%.

And the strategy is simple: instead of using the "professional headline" field to tout your particular occupational expertise — which nobody cares about — instead use this space to ask a compelling, emotional question that speaks to possible leads. Such as:

- "Need Help With Your Network Security?"
- "Looking for a Denver CPA Who'll Save You Money?"
- "Need a Dallas Financial Planner Focused on Results?"

Notice how each of these (subtly) insert a

valuable keyword in their LinkedIn profile — in a prominent spot — and ask a hot-button emotional question that a prospect already has in their head.

Trust me: If you do nothing else in this book, give this "professional headline" as a lead-generation question a try.

LinkedIn Profile Awesomeness Step #6: Create a LinkedIn Summary of Unstoppable Power

Mountains of advice have been written about how to craft the "perfect" LinkedIn profile. The only problem with much of this well-meaning advice, is that it ignores one simple fact: nobody (not even perspective employers) cares as much about your "expertise" and "experience" as you do.

So, instead I recommend you do the following with your LinkedIn profile summary:

- **Use all 2,000 characters if you can.** Don't worry, NOBODY will read the whole thing. You just want to take advantage of the plethora of keyword opportunities a long summary gives you.

- **Write your opening paragraph as if it you were writing sales copy**. Instead of dithering on about yourself in some super-boring, official way ("Big Brother, Inc. offers a full-service suite of software solutions to help businesses with their integrated HR solutions...") get right to what people care about, solving THEIR problems. (Your freebie.) "Feel like your employees spend most of their time goofing off? (While they're supposed to be doing work for you?) Get a FREE Trial to our "Big Brother" software which tracks every single thought your employees have..."

- **Share the emotional (and passionate) mission of your business.** Not just a catalog of everything clever you've ever done. Tell us WHY you're so committed to getting results for your clients and customers. (And what results you can create.) Get YOU out of the picture. (Nobody cares!)

- **Tell non-boring stories.** It's okay to put personality in your summary. (Please do!) Tell 'em about things you've learned — follow that old "Problem, Action, Result" formula every job counselor told ya about. Just be human and passionate about your business. (Chances are, total strangers will be too.)

- **Break up them paragraphs**. For the love of all that is good and true, PLEASE break up those paragraphs to a maximum of two or three sentences. And throw in a couple super-short sentences. (Helps the pacing of your summary.)

- **Break up your entire summary with subheads.** This is just a simple ALL CAPS heading to break up different aspects of your summary. (Use strange characters such as asterisks and brackets if you like.) This helps the readability of your summary. (Also helps get in some keywords.)

- **Use a primary keyword (at least twice) in your summary, and 2-3 related keywords.** You probably already know this, but it's important to get relevant keywords in your summary. But don't just settle for that ONE keyword to rule them all, go for related keywords so you can grab people no matter how they're searching.

- **Add visual content that supports the message of your business.** Great things to include would be YouTube videos, SlideShare presentations, photos of you and your team, case studies, reports…anything you can think of that would break up all that laborious text and give attention span-challenged folks a chance to check out your stuff…visually. (All you gotta do is add the link and LinkedIn will dynamically pull the info.)

- **Put in your contact info.** This is one many marketers neglect to do with their summary. But contacting people through LinkedIn email can be a pain — so if you want to hear from prospective clients and customers, throw in your contact info (such as phone number and email) to make it easy for them to reach you.

- **If you're a local business, be sure to throw in your zip code and city info.** You'd be shocked how having a zip

code in your summary can help your
Google results when people search for
businesses in their area.

LinkedIn Profile Awesomeness Step #7: Fill Out the "Rest" of Your Profile Goodies

I don't want to hurt your feelings, but most people will never get "past" your summary. (Especially if they aren't considering you for a position.) And this includes areas like "skills and endorsements" and "projects" and "experience."

That doesn't mean these areas AREN'T important. You want to get your LinkedIn profile to 100% completion, otherwise you end up looking like a total tool.

But the most important element of all these random LinkedIn profile categories is….keywords! You want them in areas like your:

- **Work Experience** - Put all those key

industry buzzwords in your current and
previous occupations.

- **Skills & Endorsements** - Ask your
  friends and colleagues to help you out
  with this (Give before you get).

- **Projects** - Don't have any projects?
  Make one up that might appeal to your
  future customer. (If somebody asks you
  about it, might be time to create it.)

- **Honors & Awards** - Tread carefully
  with these. Nobody really cares about
  these. (Unless they prove how YOU can
  help them!)

And whatever you do, don't wait till you have
the "rest" of your profile set up before you dive
headlong into the LinkedIn marketing end of things.

This is definitely something you can work on as
you go. Spend the majority of your energy on your
name, professional headline, and summary. That's
where a majority of your marketing gains will come
from.

Because when you've got that ready, it'll be time to create that most rare and hardly seen item in the universe: a LinkedIn Company page that boosts the bottom line.

Chapter Two Key Takeaways:

- **Don't feel constrained by your current LinkedIn public profile URL — you can change it!** Five times, every 180 days. (Get industry and occupational keywords in there, if you can.)

- **Don't skimp on your LinkedIn profile photo.** Make it look professional, well-lit and not something you had a colleague shoot in an interrogation room.

- **Use the background photo spot to highlight your team or customers.** (Or both.) Showing humans interacting with your product or service is IDEAL.

- **Your name field is valuable real estate** — so don't waste it by putting your moniker in there. Instead, put your occupational title in there.

- **The most ninja LinkedIn tip I can give ya** is to use your professional headline not as a brag zone for your job title — but as a place to ask a compelling question your customer is dying to know the answer to.

- **Use the first paragraph of your summary not as a place to tout your expertise**, but as if it's a de facto sales letter. (Which it is.)

- **Be sure to fill your summary (and the rest of your profile fields) with plenty of industry and occupational keywords.** (It's how people will find you.)

- **Add subheadings, unusual characters, contact info and lots of paragraph breaks to your summary.** (Make it easy for your prospects to find you and reach out.)

- **Add any visual content, such as**

video, SlideShares, or pictures — to your summary. (These can turn even the most boring LinkedIn profile into a kick-ass machine of marketing awesomeness.)

Chapter 3: How to Create a LinkedIn Company Page of Total Awesomeness

"The way to get started is to quit talking and begin doing."

-Walt Disney

I have to be honest, this is a part of my own LinkedIn profile I just didn't get for years — and neglected.

Reason was I didn't check out other company pages — so why the hell should I work on mine. (What an idiot!)

That's because having a fully stocked LinkedIn company page gives you the following opportunities:

- Access to additional LinkedIn marketing goodies (that you can't get otherwise)
- A chance to put a spotlight on your best employees — and favorite customers
- A place for you to feature all your testimonials and customer feedback
- A place to persuade future partners (and cynical media members) to help take your business to the next level.

And considering your LinkedIn Company page will be the second or third search-engine result when people type in your "company name" it's worth spending time on this powerful — but often overlooked — element of LinkedIn marketing.

So, here are my 7 Keys to Building a Kick-Ass LinkedIn Company Page:

LinkedIn Company Page Key #1: Create Your Page (and Fill It With Goodness)

Creating your actual LinkedIn company page is so simple even a Kardashian could do it. (All ya gotta do is log in, head to the "companies" tab and click on the "create a company page button.")

But here are key guidelines when creating your LinkedIn company page:

- **Don't waste the "overview" and "description" part of your company page.** This is super-vital real estate. So make sure you got something that, yes, includes keywords, but is also all about SOLVING problems. (Not just making your company sound important.) Tip: The more personal and fun this part sounds — the more people will respond to it.

- **Resize that logo image before uploading.** The ideal upload size is 300 x 300 pixels. Be sure to resize this first, before uploading. Otherwise LinkedIn will make it look Minecraft-pixelated.

- **Your background image should be sized 1584 x 396.** And you could use this spot to feature: your company tag line (sorta boring, but can be effective), behind-the-scenes pics of your business, or shots of customers using your product or service. (Probably the best way to go.)

But don't spend too much time on this initial set up. Because you want to get to…

LinkedIn Company Page Key #2: Fill Thy Company Page With SEO-Friendly Showcase Pages

If you're not familiar with LinkedIn showcase

pages, it ain't your fault — they're a relatively new feature. But showcase pages are a brilliant way to squeeze keyword-awesomeness into your Company page, at the same time you get to feature various segments and/or products within your business. (Pretty much as close to a LinkedIn win-win as you can get.)

Here's what I've learned so far implementing this new(ish) LinkedIn promotional tool:

- **Creating them is su-per simple.** You head over to your company page, click on the "edit" drop-down and choose the "create a showcase page" option.

- **The username and description of your LinkedIn is supremo SEO important.** Be sure it's titled something that packs a serious search-engine punch for your business.

- **The header image for your Showcase page differs from your Company page.** I know. Confusing, right? Still you'll want to make sure your header image for your showcase page is at least 976 x 360 pixels. (And be creative with these — they can be powerful, when done right.)

- **With a FREE LinkedIn account you're limited to just 10 showcase pages.** (At least for the time being.) So, don't waste it on elements of your business that are low-priority.

- **What should you create showcase pages about?** Well…almost anything: products, services, company initiatives…any of the major pillars that make your entire business run like the well-oiled machine it is.

- **When you're done creating these showcase pages link to them from your website, and your many social media accounts.** These are wonderful little silos of company information that

shouldn't be locked up inside the
LinkedIn confines for good.

LinkedIn Company Page Key #3: Build a Company Update Schedule

Company updates are LinkedIn's version of the Facebook status update — without all the cat meme pictures. And your Company page needs them, or else your page will look as desolate as a Sears store during "Black Friday."

LinkedIn's own advice regarding company updates is good — "We recommend company updates stay authentic, relevant, and brief" — and the key with these updates is to mix with the helpful with the (subtly) promotional.

Here's what I suggest you do:

- **Plan to post 1-2 company updates per week to your company page**. I'll go over ideal posting times later in this book, but I think Tuesday and Thursday mornings are an ideal starting point.

- **Organize your company updates according to the following ratio:** 50% Helpful, How-to Stuff; 25% Genuine News About Your Company; 25% Subtle Promotional Stuff (If you post 2x a week, this would break out to four how-to updates, two news updates and two subtle promo updates.)

- **If you're promoting something, give it an "educational" spin.** Instead of saying "We launched our brand-new product. Go buy it!"…lead with, "Here's ONE thing I learned from the launch of our new product." (Win-win on both sides.)

- **Links to external content (you didn't create) is okay, in moderation**. Don't go overboard just sharing cool stuff you came across. That's what LinkedIn groups are for, this space is about your company. So mix it up with stuff you've learned and come across yourself.

- **Motivational quotes are always good if you have NO IDEA what else to share.** I think they're insipid, but everyone else likes them.

- **Company updates are perfect for getting feedback or giving stuff away.** Just make it sound collaborative, not so sales-y.

But how do I get people to actually "follow" my page so they can see these company updates? Good question...because that leads us to...

LinkedIn Company Page Key #4: Place a "Follow Me on LinkedIn" Button on

Your Website (or Wherever Else You Can Think Of)

To get people to actually "follow" your company page, and receive notifications whenever you make an update, you need to create some kind of handy-dandy button that makes it easy for people to add themselves to your LinkedIn company tribe.

Luckily, LinkedIn makes this process super-super easy. All you gotta do is:

- Head over to Developer.LinkedIn.com/Plugins/Follow-Company

- Put in the company page you want to create the button for (I'm assuming you don't want to help promote somebody else's page)

- Spit out code

- Place that code wherever you think it might help you (Including the footer of your blog posts, website sidebars, guest

blog posts, email signatures…even in
LinkedIn pulse blog posts)

Your company page follower updates may not
skyrocket overnight — but give it a couple weeks
and you'll see results before you know it.

LinkedIn Company Page Key #5: Invite Employees (and Happy Customers) to Follow Your Page

If you REALLY wanna boost your Company
page follower count, there are four key areas where
you can find would-be tribe members:

- Current employees (Gently "suggest"
  they follow your company page)
- Happy clients and customers (Skip the
  unhappy and deranged)
- Partners (Anybody you work with)
- Members of your existing LinkedIn
  network who you think might be

interested

You don't want to just spam everybody you know — or whatever innocent victims were nice enough to accept your connection invite. Just reach out to people who have a strategic link to your business.

LinkedIn Company Page Key #6: Fill Thy Company Page With Employee Wonderment (and Customer Testimonials)

Company page recommendations are exceptionally valuable, especially for finding new clients and customers on LinkedIn. But like asking somebody to watch your three chihuahuas for two weeks while you head to Hawaii, it can be a big imposition.

So, be sure to reach out to folks who genuinely have something nice to say about your business. (Or can fake it with a proper amount of begging.) And don't forget, especially with clients and customers, to ask if there's anything YOU can do for them on LinkedIn.

LinkedIn Company Page Key #7: (Optional) Buy a Little Exposure for Your Company Page

You don't have to spend a single penny on promotion to see gains from your company page. (Especially when you implement some strategies we will go over in this book.)

But there are three advanced LinkedIn company page promo strategies I would feel remiss not sharing with you:

1. **Promoted Company Updates -** We're gonna cover LinkedIn ads in a lot more detail in Chapter 7. But for now just know that if you've got an exceptionally juicy company update you're excited about — I'm

thinking freebie giveaways and promotions disguised as how-to education — then creating a couple "promoted" company updates to your ideal customer demographic wouldn't be a bad idea. (Just tread carefully with these, LinkedIn ads can be very expensive if you're not sure what you're doing.)

2. **Fiverr SEO Backlinks -** If you're not familiar with the freelance marketplace, Fiverr, let me introduce you to your new best friend. For just $5-$10 you can buy a couple of cheap "SEO" gigs that will build backlinks to whatever URL you choose. And your LinkedIn company and showcase pages are perfect for this SEO boosting on the cheap. (I like to "SEO" gigs that include "social bookmarks" and "link pyramids.") Just make sure you include those all-important SEO keywords when creating the gig.

3. **Press Releases** - I know what I said about most people NOT caring about your latest business update. But press releases serve two functions: promote your brand and build SEO link juice to your company page. So, if there's a notable company update or showcase page you'd like to highlight, think about heading over to Fiverr and have some talented (and underpaid) English major write you up a press release.

Chapter Three Key Takeaways:

- **One of the biggest keys to outfitting your LinkedIn company page** is to ensure your description and overview are filled with keyword-filled, non-sucky copy that makes your business not sound as boring as an insurance seminar.

- **There are two key photos to upload to your LinkedIn company page.** They are the logo image — which should be resized to 100x60 — and the background image — which should be resized to 646x220. Be sure the background image shows off humans (whether customers or team members) interacting with your product or service.

- **"Showcase pages" are not only a great way to feature your many product offerings** — and categorize your business sectors in ways that customers can easily find — but it's also a fantastic way to get some much-needed keywords in your LinkedIn presence.

- **To ensure your LinkedIn company page is primed for maximum non-suckiness create a "company update" schedule** that you or somebody on your team can handle. (1-2x a week, somewhere between Tuesday-Thursday is perfect.)

- **Follow a "company update" ratio of: 50% helpful stuff, 25% news about your company, and 25% subtle promo stuff.** (Make your promos subtle by indicating what you "learned" — not just what you're selling.)

- **Place a "Follow Me on LinkedIn" button on your website** to boost your follower count. Just head over to

Developer.LinkedIn/Plugins/Follow-Company to create your button.

- **Inviting employees — and happy (non-psychotic) customers — is another great way** to get followers for your company page.

- **Also ask employees and customers (who know your name) to leave "recommendations" of your business for your company page.** (Don't ask EVERYBODY — just ask those who can rave about your business, without the threat of a subpoena.)

- **Sometimes the best exposure you can get is that which you pay for.** You can create "promoted company updates" — using the LinkedIn ad platform. Or you can use the freelance marketplace Fiverr, to promote your company page (and showcase pages) with backlinks and press releases.

Chapter 4:

7 Keys to Getting 1000s of New Connections in 30 Seconds

"Everyone should build their network before they need it."

-Dave Delaney

Connections are the rocket fuel that powers the LinkedIn universe. They're really frickin' important — and it's important you create a strategy that helps you constantly build on your network of targeted connections.

And why are they so important? Well...

- You can't contact anybody who is not a 1st-degree connection to you (More on that in a second)
- Any time you make a LinkedIn update, your 1st connection folks get notified
- It's the TOLL BOOTH for reaching out to new leads and future clients on LinkedIn

Okay, great. I need some LinkedIn connections. How do I do that?

Well, before we jump in with the whole LinkedIn connection world tour, let me take a moment to make sure we are all on the same "connection" page.

How the Whole LinkedIn Connection Thang Works

Remember that whole "Six Degrees of Kevin

Bacon" game where you'd try to link any movie —
or any Hollywood star — within six degrees of the
famed star of "Footloose."

Well, LinkedIn works (sorta) the same way.

There are three degrees of connection in the
LinkedIn world:

- **1st-Degree Connection** - This is where
  you or another person have accepted an
  invitation to connect on LinkedIn. You
  can contact these people by emailing
  through LinkedIn. (People in the same
  groups as you are, are considered 1st-
  degree connections.)

- **2nd-Degree Connection** - These are
  people who are connected to YOUR
  1st-degree connections.

- **3rd-Degree Connection** - These are
  people who are connected to YOUR
  2nd-degree connections.

It isn't exactly rocket science, but your job is to

build out your 1st-degree list of connections as quickly as possible — which then puts you in a position to send out "connect" invitations to your 2nd-degrees.

Don't worry if this seems confusing — or downright pointless. There are LOTS of different ways to reach your future customers, clients and partners in the LinkedIn world. (And we're gonna go over a bunch of 'em in the chapter.)

So, let's jump right in with my 7 Keys to Getting a Crapload of LinkedIn Connections:

LinkedIn Connection Key #1: Have Something to Offer

Wait…what? Aren't I supposed to just send out spammy LinkedIn connection requests?

Well, yes, you could do that. (And most everybody else does.)

Or you could have something special you give away to new connections and find your connection request success rates jump by 50-60%.

Now this "something" you're offering doesn't have to be extensive, or the complete 100-page guide to "anything."

It could be your #1 ninja-hack strategy secret thing-a-majiggy that you think your ideal customer on LinkedIn would take advantage of. Or it could simply be a LinkedIn connection-only coupon or discount. (Or if you're selling more high-ticket items, it could be a free consultation.)

What's key is that ONCE you have your free thing nailed down, you want to go back in and add a reference to the FREEBIE in the first line of the "summary" of your LinkedIn profile.

Example:

"If you'd like to discover my #1 Secret Insider Tip for Keeping LinkedIn From Sending You 1200 Emails a Day…then connect with me on LinkedIn and I'll send it over to ya."

Why do things this way?

Because when somebody gets your "connection

request" the first thing they will do is check out your profile.

And if your "summary" text is all about what YOU can do for THEM — instead of a laundry list of your accomplishments — they are much more likely to connect with you. (And start what might hopefully be a profitable — and beautiful — friendship.)

LinkedIn Connection Key #2: Make Sure Thy Profile is Complete

This should go without saying. But so should the dangers of "backyard wrestling." (And yet people still do it.)

- Before you send out your 100s of "Hey! Let's connect on LinkedIn" emails, take a moment to fill out all your key profile elements. That includes:
- Profile picture
- Background picture

- Name (Which includes your name and title)
- Professional headline (Which includes your hot-button question your prospective customers need help with)
- Summary (Which includes a reference to your freebie for LinkedIn connections and plenty of keyword awesomeness.)

This doesn't have to be perfect. But you want to get it looking like you give a crap what people think on LinkedIn.

LinkedIn Connection Key #3: Reach Out to Your Inner Circle

I'm not gonna spend much time on this — because chances are you've already done this.

But in case you didn't do this when you created your account — send "connect requests" to folks you already know. (And by "already know" — I mean people who would instantly recognize your name if it showed up in their email.)

Don't worry if they don't get back to you right away. (LinkedIn sends out so much damn spam, it can take a while for people to get back to you.)

But at the least you want to reach out to:

- Email contacts (This is usually done automatically for you upon account creation)
- Employees (past and current)
- Customers (past and current)
- Die-hard social media fans (they call these evangelists, I think)

So what do you say when you approach the folks? Well, whatever you do, try NOT to use the generic "I'd like to add you to my professional network." (Sounds as robotic as a Presidential debate.)

Instead add in your own personality. (And show the person you're sending the request to that you took an extra 12 seconds to write something just for them.)

For example, if I'm reaching out to somebody I've worked with in the past, but who may not recall just who the hell I am, I'll do something like:

"Hi there,

"I don't know if you remember me, but (Insert reason for connection: "We did some contracting work for you a few years back"; "We got stuck in an elevator last week for 27 straight hours") and I wanted to add you to my professional network.

"If you prefer not to connect for any reason please click "Ignore" instead of "I don't know this person." Thanks so much!"

The keys to this request are 1) I tell them HOW we're connected (not force them to figure it out) and 2) I ask them to select "Ignore" instead of "Don't Know."

This is because LinkedIn keeps track of the number of people who claim they DON'T know you. And if you send too many requests to people you DON'T know, LinkedIn will cap the number of requests you get to send out. (No bueno.)

Now, for folks who will recognize your name right away, get more conversational and intimate with your request.

"Hey Kim Kardashian,

How have you been? Sounds like you've had a busy couple years. What with being married to Kanye West — good luck with that — and being one of the most famous people in the world despite having not a single ounce of talent."

Let's connect on LinkedIn. (Just don't send me a copy of your book.)

Talk soon

LinkedIn Connection Key #4: Become a Thriving (Productive) Member of 5 LinkedIn Groups

In the next chapter I'm going to cover the somewhat-strange — but very effective — strategy of creating (and running) your own LinkedIn group. (Easier than you think; more profitable too.)

But for now, here's what you GOTTA know about LinkedIn Groups:

- **LinkedIn Groups are STILL one of the best ways to find new connections**. No matter how many ways people try to screw it up.

- **Ya gotta be an active member to get much benefit**. That means liking, commenting and sharing way MORE than promoting.

- **It's better to focus all your energies on 4-5 groups, than split your efforts on 15-20 groups.** This one took me forever to figure out, but, trust me, the real benefits come from focused group activity — not a shotgun approach to promotion.)

- **If you can only check in a couple times a week, make sure it's Tuesday through Thursday**. These are when most people are on LinkedIn.

- **Don't overly promote.** For every blatant promotional update you share — and some groups may not even allow this — try to have 3-4 status updates that offer advice or help others out.

- **Learn the lay of the land before posting a ton.** Each LinkedIn group has its own schedules and tendencies. Join 4-5 groups and just observe for a couple weeks before making any demands.

- **To find groups where your ideal customers are hanging out, put in keywords related to your industry in the "Groups" search engine.** Don't worry if you must wait for approval. It's often worth it.

- **Spend time "commenting" and "liking" other people's stuff each week**. And by "commenting" I mean more than just "Thx!"

LinkedIn Connection Key #5: Collect Your "Magic 100"

The "Magic 100" is more than just a vague term I made up because I wasn't creative enough to come up with something more exciting.

It's a targeted list of LinkedIn users you'd LOVE to add to your network. This could include future:

- Customers and/or clients
- Partners
- Vendors
- Journalists
- Bloggers
- Podcast producer
- Industry governing bodies
- Anybody who could move the needle on your business
- To create your "Magic 100" all ya gotta do is:

- Open a text document in your text editor of choice (I use "Notepad")
- Make a list of occupations that are relevant to your ideal customer. These includes terms such as "owner," "reporter," "founder," "Head of the Jedi Council."
- Make a list of industry-specific keywords. Such as "restaurant," "plumbing," "dental," "light saber technician."
- Head over to the LinkedIn search bar and put in different combinations that incorporate one occupation and one industry keyword (all in quotes) — with the word "AND" (all in caps) between them. Examples: "pizza" AND "owner"; "partner" AND "law firm"; "Sith Lord" AND "Galactic Empire."
- Scan these search results — bookmark them as well — and add anybody who

you want to reach out to in your handy-
dandy Excel sheet (or some other word
processor that doesn't feature a paper
clip as its mascot.)

Now you don't have to limit yourself to just 100.
You could do 1,000. Or 12 billion. (Although that
may take a while.)

But it's good to have a tangible goal to build up
your army of future LinkedIn connections. Which
we'll need when we work with…

LinkedIn Connection Key #6: Create a Weekly "Connection Request" Schedule

Once you've got your profile looking sharp, and
you've joined some groups — and have your list of
"Magic 100," it's time to begin the methodical
(though often profitable) process of reaching out to
(somewhat) strangers and asking them to join your
network.

Now, how much "connection requesting" you're willing to do will depend on your schedule. And how many college-age interns you've got in your own "Galactic Empire" but my own connection request schedule looks something like this:

- **Monday 8am** — 3 connection requests to fellow members of Group #1; 3 connection requests to "Magic 100 bloggers"

- **Tuesday 8am** — 3 connection requests to fellow members of Group #2; 3 connection requests to "Magic 100 future clients/customers"

- **Wednesday 8am** — 3 connection requests to fellow members of Group #3; 3 connection requests to "Magic 100 journalists"

- **Thursday 8am** — 3 connection requests to fellow members of Group #4; 3 connection requests to "Magic 100 future clients/customers"

- **Friday 8am** — 3 connection requests to fellow members of Group #5; 3 connection requests to "Magic 100 future partners"

Now you could do more than this. (And I usually do.) Or you could organize WHO you target differently.

You may have no interest in partners — and instead may want to focus 100% of your energies on future customers and clients.

But try to come up with some minimum weekly amount of requests that hit all the MAJOR pillars of your overall LinkedIn promotion marketing plan.

And when you send out your connection request, I recommend you use the following template:

"Hi There,

My name is Michael Clarke. I'm the founder of Punk Rock Marketing (Insert reason you found them: "I noticed an update you shared in a group we belong to"; "I found you in a

LinkedIn search I was doing) and I'd like to add you to my professional network.

If you prefer not to connect for any reason, please click "Ignore" instead of "I don't know this person." Thanks so much!

P.S. Please don't report this as spam."

Again, you want to tell them

- Who you are
- How you found them
- That you'd prefer they click on "Ignore" over "I don't know this person."

And that's it!

Trust me: If you keep sending these out, week-by-week, and use the customized (non-generic) templates we've gone over — besides checking in with your LinkedIn groups a couple times ago — you'll see such a response rate you'll wonder what ELSE can I do to broaden my LinkedIn network. (Which is what we'll tackle in the next chapter.)

Chapter 4 Key Takeaways

• **The LinkedIn network is organized by degrees of connection.** (1st-degree connections are those who've accepted your invite to connect; 2nd-degree connections are those connected to your 1st-degrees; 3rd-degree connections are those connected to your 2nd-degrees.)

• **The #1 key to getting more connections is to have something to offer new connections.** Doesn't have to be big — just a small thing you think connections would like.

• **Make sure your profile is complete before you go searching for new connections.** (This includes all the typical stuff — summary, job experience — but also those pesky background pictures that everybody forgets about.)

- **Reaching out to people you KNOW is the easiest way to build your network.** This includes employees, customers, social media fans, and email contacts. (Just be sure to make that LinkedIn invite personal. No robotic queries!)

- **One of the fastest ways to build your LinkedIn network** is to become a kick-ass member of five LinkedIn groups. (Don't join 50. Stick with five and go from there.)

- **Creating a "Magic 100" list of folks you'd like to connect with is a great way to build your network** — and your profit margin. This includes future clients, partners and vendors — besides bloggers, journalists and industry experts who can spread your message at light-speed.

- **The best way to ensure consistent**

building of your network is to schedule your sending of weekly connection requests. I like to do three fellow group members and three off the Magic 100 — each Monday-Friday. But whatever you choose, go with a schedule you can keep to. (You'll see great results if you do.)

Chapter 5:

Blatant Profiteer's Guide to Creating (and Running) LinkedIn Groups

"The single greatest 'people skill' is a highly-developed and authentic interest in the other person."

-Bob Burg

Huh? Create and run a LinkedIn group?

I'm sure you need ONE MORE THING to manage in your business like you need a tax audit.

But "owning" your own LinkedIn group offers you a ton of super-ninja marketing benefits:

- **Your number of connections will go through the roof** — There is just no better way to connect with new people than a LinkedIn group)

- **You'll become an authority in your industry** — Even if you don't have the certification — or standing — to be an authority

- **You'll drive traffic to your website** — Or wherever you send folks

- **It's a helluva lot easier to get media attention** when you run a LinkedIn group

- **You get to send out a weekly message to EVERY single person in the group** — Huge game-changer!

And it's that last one where I think the real gains of a LinkedIn group can be found. I have a feeling LinkedIn groups are gonna be the "new" email newsletter. (Or at least how email newsletters used to be back in the Mesozoic era of 1997.)

If you could send out a weekly email to 2500-5000 leads — that you didn't have to pay for — would you do it? (Hell yeah!)

Well, LinkedIn groups can offer that to ya. But you gotta set things up right. (And spend time each week cultivating that LinkedIn group.)

But if you can get past the initial growing pains, running a successful LinkedIn group might be the most lucrative promotional vehicle you can have.

But enough of the talk, let's jump right in with my 5 Pillars of a Profitable LinkedIn Group:

Profitable LinkedIn Group Pillar #1: Brainstorm Ways to Serve Your Industry (NOT Just Ways to Sell 'Em Stuff)

Oh, I know you want to sell 'em stuff. (And you will, trust me.) But your initial objective with your LinkedIn group should be more altruistic.

All ya gotta do is reverse-engineer the process.

Ask yourself: "Why do I join groups in the first place?" Generally it comes down to you committing to:

- Make new connections
- Figure out how to make your business more profitable
- Promote something

So, whether you organize your group by occupation ("Long Island Plumbing Network") or by industry ("Direct Response Advertiser Collective") or some other demographic ("League of Extraordinary San Diego Marketers") try to come up with a compelling reason WHY the group should exist. (And find a name that attracts your ideal customer.)

Profitable LinkedIn Group Pillar #2: Create Your Group for Maximum Awesomeness

Creating the group is simple. (Just select "Groups" from the navigation, and then click on "My Groups." You'll then see a prompt for "Create a group.")

But there are a few things to keep in mind as you fill out the group's information to completion:

- **Keywords are gold -** You'll want to include them in your Group Name, Summary and Description. And these aren't necessarily Google-friendly keywords — though that can certainly be helpful — but these should be LinkedIn keywords (such as occupation and industry) that people are likely to use to find your group. (Not sure what keywords to use? Just find out what other groups are using to get ideas.)

- **Your summary should be both description and an invitation to join** - The summary is the "short description" of what your Group is all about. And that's important. But you also want to tell people what they need to do to join the group. The question is do you want to have to "approve" everybody who wants to join the group. (I recommend you do.) If that's the way you want to go, then just put in some text that says something like "Join group to apply for membership." (This lets them know they have to hit "join" — but that membership isn't guaranteed.)

- **The description is your long (ish) detailing of what you'll cover in the group -** Don't worry not everybody is gonna read this entire thing. You just want to put enough description — and enough keywords — to give people an idea of what they can expect from joining the group.

- **Be sure to upload a logo image that's no bigger than 100 x 60 pixels -** I know, that's tiny. But these are rules as delivered upon high, so to make sure your image doesn't get horribly manipulated, give the LinkedIn police exactly what they want.

- **Under website, choose a URL that promotes opt-ins** — Don't send people to your homepage. (Unless your homepage is stocked and ready to convert.) Instead, put in a link to a page that can offer your freebie — and collect a lead at the same time.

Profitable LinkedIn Group Pillar #3:
Set Some Ground Rules

This is where the real challenge in managing a group comes — making sure other people don't ruin it with their spammy or abusive comments.

Now, most people will be perfectly polite citizens in your LinkedIn group domain, but there are always a few loons who see it as their LinkedIn-given right to do whatever the hell they want.

Luckily, LinkedIn allows you to set "group rules" for your little patch of LinkedIn real estate. This is where you lay down what you will — and will not — allow in your group.

I've actually created a template for you to use; you can grab your totally FREE LinkedIn Group rules template over at: PunkRockMarketing.com/GroupRules.

But no matter how you style your particular "group rules" make sure you have at the least the following:

- Make sure people post in English. Unless your Group caters to a non-English-speaking audience. This isn't xenophobia, this is to combat spam.

- Always insist on respectful comments. Otherwise this can get out of hand.

- Insist on relevance. A post on Digital Marketing has no place in a Group dedicated to D&D players. Encourage people to keep things focused.

- Be clear that promotions and job postings belong in the "promotions" and "jobs" tabs. This will probably be the #1 bane of your LinkedIn group existence. (And a little leeway can be allowed.) But you want to avoid your group being over-run by shameless promoters. (Like yourself.)

- Encourage people to share their insights, knowledge and opinions. Tell 'em you want them to share what's going on — just to do it in a respectful, non-spammy way.

Profitable LinkedIn Group Pillar #4: Create a Weekly Posting Schedule

So the real "job" of running a LinkedIn Group — aside from keeping the spam robots from hijacking the enterprise — is to come up with some kind of regular posting schedule that will keep the Group from dying on the vine.

Now how often you post — and what you post — will depend on your particular industry. (And how much time you have to devote to the Group.)

But here are a few guidelines that have worked for me regarding the what, when and how of posting to LinkedIn Groups:

- **1-2x a week is ideal.** With once a week being an absolute minimum.
- **Tuesday - Thursday is your sweet spot in terms of LinkedIn Group**

activity. So if you will only post a couple times a week try to have it be in that time range.

- **The best time of day to share is 7am-8am…maybe.** This will depend highly on who you're trying to reach. If your ideal customer segment is corporate — and they're likely to be in front of their desks all day — then mornings are great. But if your ideal audience is on service calls all day, then post in that 5pm-6pm range.

- **Don't just share links.** Mix up the kinds of stuff you share: quotes, insights, discussion topics, blog posts, videos, slideshares, infographics.

- **Keep your ratio of posts to 80% industry-related helpful stuff, and 20% promotional stuff.** This is a good rule for any kind of social media platform but do your best not to violate this rule.

So, for example, here is a monthly posting schedule for one of my LinkedIn Groups:

- **Week One:** Tues morning (Blog Post Link); Thurs morning (Question of the week)
- **Week Two:** Tues morning (Infographic/Visual Content Link); Thurs morning (Question of the week)
- **Week Three:** Tues morning (Video Link); Thurs morning (Question of the week)
- **Week Four:** Tues morning (News Item Link); Thurs morning (Question of the week)

Now your particular posting schedule may look different. But you'll notice I mix up the TYPES of stuff I shared in my LinkedIn group — not all boring 5000-word essays.

I also tend to post my "Questions of the week"

on Thursdays. (This is because people's brain-cell capacity for consuming content tends to go down as the week goes on — but their ability to share their opinion never wavers.)

However you slice it, if you stick with a rough schedule like this one, you'll ensure your LinkedIn Group stays as vibrant — and helpful — as possible.

Profitable LinkedIn Group Pillar #5: Create a Weekly Maintenance Schedule

And by "maintenance" I simply mean checking on your LinkedIn group. Making comments. Removing any offensive posts. Keeping the spam to a minimum.

Again this doesn't — and shouldn't — take hours of your time up each week. But in my experience, unless this is scheduled, it'll never happen.

So, here's what my weekly maintenance schedule looks like:

- Tuesday Evening (5 mins)
- Thursday Evening (5 mins)
- Saturday Morning (5 mins)

You'll notice I do my posting in the mornings, but I do my maintenance in the evenings. This lets me a) respond to any comments or questions I got from my earlier posts and b) manage any weird stuff that comes up.

Also, though I know Saturdays aren't big LinkedIn consumption times, it's good to take just a few minutes on the weekend to make sure things are looking good. (And free of zombie spammers.)

Profitable LinkedIn Group Pillar #6: Come Up With a Weekly Email Schedule

So this is where LinkedIn Groups get exciting. (And really profitable.) And that is by sending out "LinkedIn group announcements" you control — and that get delivered right into your group member's inbox.

Now you're limited to ONE announcement per week. (But really sending more than one of these per week will get really annoying, really fast.)

And what should you promote in these announcements? Well, you could promote all kinds of things:

- Content you created
- A survey you hope folks take
- A freebie offer (probably the most effective thing you can promote in these announcements)
- A special, limited-time offer (just for members of the group)
- An affiliate product (you've actually used and that you highly recommend)
- Anything you think could help members of your group (and perhaps also your bank account)

I don't recommend you promote stuff people

have to pay for EVERY single week. (You'll get a ton of churn in your LinkedIn group.) But I think promoting something people can buy, 1-2x month, is fine.

And what should you put in these announcements? Well, I think, at the very least, you need:

- A quick note about why you're writing them (and why it's IMPORTANT they read on)
- A call-to-action (with hyperlink) of what they should do next
- A brief breakdown of the benefits if they click on the link and act
- A "What do you think about this topic? Leave a comment below!" piece at the end

Here's an example to show you what this might look like in real-life:

"Hey Small Biz Ninjas,

We all know analytics are vitally important to running a successful business. (It's just that they're so dang confusing — if not monumentally boring.)

That's why I've put together a super-quick cheat sheet called "The 5 Metrics EVERY Business Must Track (and How to Set 'Em Up)" which you can grab TOTALLY FREE!

Just head over to: PunkRockMarketing.com/AnlayticsAreBoring

In it you'll get a down-and-dirty guide to learning:

- *How to track where your web traffic is coming from (Even social media!)*
- *How to set up analytics goals that ACTUALLY affect your business*
- *And how to set up actual profit projections — not just guesses — for your business*

Did I mention it's free?

By the way, I'd love to know WHICH metrics you think are most important for your business? Share in the comments below!

Michael Clarke"

The reason we want to add the whole "What do ya think" angle is that when you schedule the announcement, you will be able to turn it into a "featured discussion." (Which you wanna do! You want your promo stuff to become somewhat "viral," if it can.)

And as for WHEN to send these announcements? That will depend entirely upon your particular corner of the business universe. But generally I like to send these out early Saturday mornings. (Less competition on the weekends.)

But do some testing. See what works for you. And be sure to use this most valuable aspect of LinkedIn Group management.

Profitable LinkedIn Group Pillar #7: Build an Army of Group Members

Many of the strategies we've gone over earlier, in

building our network of connections and gathering company page followers, can also be applied to building up one kick-ass LinkedIn group.

But just in case aliens wiped the hard drive of your brain…err…you may not have memorized every word I put to paper, here are a couple of no-brainer people to reach out to build your LinkedIn Group member count:

- Members of your existing network (who might benefit from the group)
- Fellow members of other LinkedIn groups you belong to
- Clients/customers
- Vendors
- Partners
- Influencers/Media
- Employees/Colleagues
- Anyone on your "Magic 100" — the list of folks you'd like to be connected with
- Experts in your industry
- Subscribers to your email list

- And to promote your LinkedIn group to the big-bad Internet universe, you could do a few no-brainer things: (Most of which can be outsourced to a freelancer on Fiverr)
- Publish a press release about the group
- Share featured group posts on Facebook, Twitter, and Google+
- Buy SEO backlinks to the URL of your LinkedIn Group
- Put links to your LinkedIn Group page on your website, blog, business card, etc.

The cool thing is if you do just a few of the promotional things I've mentioned — and you see steady growth in the popularity of your group — LinkedIn will definitely meet you half-way.

And before you know it LinkedIn will feature you in their prized search-engine results, and you'll see so much free traffic (and additional group members) that you'll have more connections, subscribers and customers than you'll know what to do with.

And that, my friends, is a "group" all of us would love to spend time in.

Chapter 5 Key Takeaways:

- **Creating and running your own LinkedIn Groups are a fantastic way to find new clients and customers on LinkedIn.** (And the author thinks they will eventually become the "new" email list of the future.)

- **When creating a LinkedIn Group, brainstorm ways of creating a resource for others.** (Not just an excuse to promote your crap.)

- **Fill out the vital details of your LinkedIn Group** — and that includes the summary, title and description — with plenty of keyword goodness.

- **You gotta set ground rules for your Group before you get the ball rolling.** To get my sample template of LinkedIn Group rules head over to: PunkRockMarketing.com/GroupRules

- **To keep your Group vibrant — and full of lead-generating activity — create a weekly posting schedule.** (1-2x a week is ideal, with a mix of how-to-stuff, discussion topics, and promo stuff.)

- **To keep your Group from being overrun** with hijacked discussions and spammy users, set aside time for LinkedIn Group Maintenance. (Just 5 mins, 3 days a week should do)

- **You can send ONE email a week** to members of your LinkedIn Group. (Be sure to take advantage.) Share insights, content, resource guides, and at least 1x a month something you're selling.

- **To build up your army of LinkedIn Group members** reach out to employees, colleagues, vendors, customers and clients. (Ask what you can do for them.)

Chapter 6:

How to Use LinkedIn Pulse for Complete (and Total) World Domination

"Adapt what is useful, reject what is useless, and use what is specifically your own."

-Bruce Lee

It's possible this entire chapter will be irrelevant to your business.

You may NOT have any use for content marketing — the practice by which you create a piece of content in the hopes this content will bring your business exposure (and hopefully additional leads.)

And you may have even less interest in taking the time to CREATE a piece of content that lives on the LinkedIn servers.

But having worked with clients in businesses whose target audience you wouldn't think would be receptive to content marketing — such as the craft beer industry and the carpet-cleaning mafia — I can just say...you'd be surprised how powerful content marketing is.

Because there may be no more powerful force in this universe than the need to NOT feel dumb — and feel SMARTER than everybody else.

And you sharing your expertise — in whatever field — is a fast-track way to win the hearts, minds (and wallets) of your ideal customer.

And as for your content "living" on somebody else's real estate...I hate to break it to ya...but I think the days of people visiting individual websites to consume content are gonna go the way of Lindsay

Lohan's career.

So, before you poo-poo using content marketing — and specifically the LinkedIn Pulse platform — keep an open mind and give this method a chance. You might just be shocked how powerful (and profitable) it really can be.

Okay, so let's jump right in with my LinkedIn Pulse Marketing FAQ:

LinkedIn Pulse Marketing FAQ #1: Just What the Hell is "LinkedIn Pulse?"

LinkedIn Pulse — yeah, I hate the name too — is LinkedIn's dedicated content platform in which users can publish content using a variety of mediums — text, video, images, SlideShares, cave paintings, etc.

LinkedIn Pulse was originally an invite-only platform. Meaning you had to wait for an invite from Richard Branson — hey, Richard, I'm still waiting

for a ride on the jet — to use it. But now it's
available to all LinkedIn users.

LinkedIn Pulse Marketing FAQ #2: How Is Pulse Different From Regular Content Marketing?

Simple…the content LIVES on LinkedIn.
(Meaning you can't control its placement and you
can't retarget to consumers of that content later on.)

But the advantages outweigh the disadvantages:

- Your post will rank MUCH higher in
  the search engines
- Your post will be accessible in the
  LinkedIn search engine
- Your post will have the chance to be
  discovered by a much-larger audience
  (especially media)
- Your post (if it gets momentum behind
  it) will be put in "LinkedIn Spotlight"
  (which can get you thousands of readers

in no time)

Just so you know, I struggled with the whole "publish on my site or publish on LinkedIn" debate?

And I would say, if you think a good portion of your target audience is already on LinkedIn AND you're trying to establish your expertise with your marketing — not just a faster, cheaper, better mousetrap — then I would encourage you strongly to focus a good portion of your energies on creating content for LinkedIn Pulse.

LinkedIn Pulse Marketing FAQ #3: What Should I Write My Pulse Articles About?

Well, first off, you don't have to necessarily "write" anything. There are plenty of other modalities — such as video, image or SlideShare — that you can use to create "Pulse" content.

But I love you're asking the question FIRST — not after you've already created the content.

Many clients I work with, who've tried "Pulse" with virtually no success, have encountered problems because they didn't brainstorm strategically their content before creating.

So, here's a quick step-by-step guide to creating killer "Pulse" content:

1. **Search "Pulse" for topic ideas.** Why do all the heavy-lifting yourself? Just search the "pulse" platform — type in your industry — and see what other topics people have covered. (Tip: If you still can't find anything, check the Table of Contents of books in your industry on Amazon. Those are a treasure trove of ideas.)

2. **Determine your target audience (and what end results you'd like them to have).** I know you might think you have ONE audience — but I'm sure within that one audience you have different segments. So, decide WHO exactly this content is for — and what end result/insight you'd like

them to come away with.

3. **Group your "Pulse" post into logical sub-headings.** This will likely be the "three steps" or "five keys" or " seven big takeaways" related to your topic. (You'll notice I do this shamelessly throughout this book. That's cos it works.)

4. **Come up with a schnazzy title that would get noticed on a smartphone.** Pretend like you're a 22-year-old intern/journalist working for one of those "clickbait" farms like BuzzFeed. What kind of compelling title could you come up with? ("5 Things Every Contractor Needs to Know About the New Tax Laws"; "How to Not Royally Suck at Your First Radio Interview.") Make it sound fun — even if the topic is dry.

5. **Write the damn thing.** Don't feel like just because it's LinkedIn you gotta make your content sound all official and business-y.

Write in a conversational tone like you talk. Your content — and your marketing message — will be received much better if you can.

LinkedIn Pulse Marketing FAQ #4: How Do I Publish on LinkedIn Pulse?

The actual mechanics of your posting on "Pulse" are super easy. All you do is:

- Click on "Interests" (top navigation)
- Select "Pulse"
- Select "Publish a Post"
- And type (or paste) in your textual LinkedIn goodness

But let me give you a couple rules-of-the-road to ensure your post gets the maximum amount of awesomeness possible.

- **Put a call-to-action in your footer and a LINK to your website in the**

body of your post. Your footer call-to-action can be your usual standard "If you'd like more information, head over to…blah…blah…blah." But the real SEO benefit will be in putting a keyword (linked to your website) in the body of your post.

- **Insert at least 2-3 images in your post.** The longer your post, the more images you should have. (Optimal amount seems to be seven, but that seems like a lot more work than I'm willing to do.)

- **Add any relevant video, SlideShares and infographics to your post.** Doesn't have to be stuff you created. (I love throwing YouTube videos in my posts — if only to break up the monotony.) Just try to use "rich media" to boost your "likes" and "shares."

- **Add plenty of headings (h2 button)**

to separate content. This not only makes your content easier to read — but also provides extra SEO juice to your headings. (So, if you can get a keyword in there...do it!)

- **Add lots of relevant tags when publishing.** This will help the discoverability of your post.

- **Publishing on "Pulse" is a cumulative effect.** Don't freak out if you don't see results instantly. It is a long-term, though effective, strategy.

LinkedIn Pulse Marketing FAQ #5: How Do I Promote My Pulse Article?

The short answer is: any damn well way you can. But a couple of my favorite go-to ways to promote "Pulse" posts include sharing with:

- LinkedIn groups you belong to (or manage)

- Followers of your company page
- Any notable LinkedIn connections (including media)
- Twitter followers
- Facebook fans
- Email subscribers
- Google+ plus-ers

In addition, if you wanted to get super-ninja about your "Pulse" promotion, you could:

- Publish a press release
- Post an excerpt on your blog
- Buy backlinks to the post (with Fiverr)
- Take out a few Facebook (or LinkedIn) ads
- Share it on Quora (as an answer to an existing question)
- Share it in any message boards or forums you belong to

There's virtually no limit on the many ways you can promote your "Pulse" posts. (And once ya get a buzz going, LinkedIn will take over from there.)

LinkedIn Pulse Marketing FAQ #6: How Often Should I Publish on "Pulse"?

There's no hard-and-fast rule to this. (Unfortunately.) The more you publish, the more chances you give your future clients and customers to find you.

But you do lean more toward quality than quantity. (No point in churning out three mediocre posts a week, when one really good post would prove more beneficial.)

In my experience, publishing ONE quality "Pulse" post a week is usually all you need to accomplish your goals. (Besides you don't want to over-saturate your network with constant "look at me!" content promotion.)

What I would recommend you do, however, is to write about 3-4 of these before you start publishing. (This will give you a month of regular "Pulse" content, which will give you time to test and tweak different promotion methods to see what works best.)

And there's no question LinkedIn rewards content producers who are consistent. And if you show — right out of the gate — that you aren't a total slacker, you'll have a much higher likelihood of getting a future "Pulse" post featured by the LinkedIn gods.

Which just might get you that much closer to a weekend invite from Mr. Branson.

Chapter 6 Key Takeaways:

- **"LinkedIn Pulse" is a powerful — if oddly named - content marketing platform** in which you create content that lives on the LinkedIn servers.

- **Yes, it's scary to create content for real estate you don't control**, but the author is skeptical about how viable company websites will be in the future.

- **The best way to figure out what to create content "about" is to research** what's already been covered on "Pulse." (OR check out Amazon book "Table of Contents" for suggestions.)

- **When you publish your content to "Pulse" don't forget** to add any relevant videos, SlideShares, or photos. (Breaks up all that text.)

- **Promote your "Pulse" articles to whoever you think might be**

benefited. This includes: fellow LinkedIn group members, social media fans, notable LinkedIn connections, Lady Gaga, etc.

- **Publishing 1-2x a week is ideal.** (More than that and you risk over-saturating your audience.)

Chapter 7:

Your Super-Quick Guide to LinkedIn Ads That Don't Suck

"Creative without strategy is called 'art.' Creative with strategy is called 'advertising.'"

-Jeff I. Richards

Before we jump into the strange (though often profitable) world of LinkedIn ads, I have to be upfront with you.

Though I love LinkedIn ads, and recommend

them for all my B2B clients using LinkedIn, the platform is so new I am by no means the ultimate LinkedIn ads expert.

But having organized a few hundred of these campaigns, for both myself and my clients, I'm pretty jazzed about the potential that LinkedIn ads gives us as marketers.

That's because:

- LinkedIn ads are still the best — and most reliable — source of social media lead-generation around. (Way better than Twitter or Facebook — the key is to make sure it's at a price you can live with.)
- No other ad platform offers the occupational, educational and company targeting that LinkedIn ads do.
- LinkedIn ads offer the fantastic ability for users to choose the option of having you "follow up" with them personally.

Now as with any advertising platform, the key is to make sure the cost of lead acquisition fits comfortably within the goals of your funnel. (No amount of fuzzy math will make up for the fact that LinkedIn ads are on the expensive side.)

But if you know WHO you want to reach — and you've got a message you're fairly certain will resonate — then LinkedIn ads offer you a unique opportunity in the digital marketing world: cut through the bullshit and communicate directly with the decision-makers of companies all over the world.

So, with that "caveat emptor" out of the way, let's jump right in with my 5 Keys to LinkedIn Advertising Awesomeness:

LinkedIn Advertising Key #1: Figure Out HOW MUCH You're Willing to Spend

There are two (somewhat) daunting facts about LinkedIn advertising:

- The minimum CPC bid is $2.00. (And that doesn't guarantee placement, that's just the minimum.)
- The minimum daily budget is $10/day or $300/month.

And though this may induce zombie apocalypse level anxiety in even the most confident marketer as long as you know what you're willing to spend — both on a daily scale and total campaign level — then you'll be less likely to encounter "sticker shock" when the ads run.

In my experience this all comes down to what a single lead is worth to you. (And what your current lead-acquisition costs are.)

Generally I recommend marketers budget at least a minimum of $100 in their total ad spend with their initial LinkedIn ad campaign. This will give you enough information to find out if:

1. Your offer resonates with folks when they click on your ad

2.   Your ad grabs the attention of the LinkedIn universe.

Once you've got a winner — or at least something that is converting at a rate you are comfortable with — it's just a matter of scaling it up.

But stick with the minimum $10/day daily budget at first. (No need to burn through your budget until you've got a handle on how your ad is performing.)

LinkedIn Advertising Key #2: Decide on What Type of Ad to Run

There are two kinds of ads you can run on the LinkedIn ad platform — although if you eventually become a LinkedIn partner you get a bunch of other advertising options. (But if your business is at that level, chances are you're not reading this book right now.)

The two most common types of LinkedIn ads are:

- **Sponsored content** - Where you boost an existing status update made by your profile, group or company page. Best results from this one, especially with content.

- **Dynamic Ads** - Where you deliver personalized ads in the sidebar that send people to your website. Good, if they convert. Expensive if they don't.

- **Text Ads** - Like they sound, short text ads with a small picture. You only pay for clicks you get, so can be a good strategy. But won't send a ton of traffic your way.

- **Sponsored InMail** - I have not had good success with these. So, I can't recommend them. Maybe you'll do better than I did. In which case email me and let me know.

In my experience, unless you're selling REALLY big-ticket items and need just a few leads to make the numbers work, the "sponsored updates" don't always pay off in the long run.

This will depend on your particular funnel. But these kinds of "content-type" ads can get expensive, fast.

Instead, I recommend — especially if this is your first time out with LinkedIn ads — you start off with display ads. (Which entice users to click on your ad to be taken to a web page of your choosing.)

Now as for whether to go with video or text, the data I've collected seems to suggest that text ads convert better. I know this is counter to the whole "everything is going mobile and visual" mantra that surrounds marketing.

But from what I've found, LinkedIn is something people STILL do at work, in a professional setting. (And putting on headphones so they can listen to you yammer on for three minutes isn't always the best way to entice prospects.)

But you'll want to do your own testing to see what works for you. And if you've already got a well-converting video, that's crushing it on other ad platforms, such as Facebook, then definitely explore putting this video up on LinkedIn.

LinkedIn Advertising Key #3: Nail Down WHAT You Want to Promote

I know this'll sound wishy-washy, but again this will depend on YOUR business. But my recommendation is to always send "cold" advertising traffic to an email opt-in page.

That's because:

- Opt-in pages convert better than sales page with "cold" traffic
- Sending "cold" traffic to opt-in pages lets you retarget those folks — even if they don't opt-in — on platforms like Google or Facebook

Now what this opt-in page looks like will depend on what you're asking people to sign up for.

If it's a simple PDF case study or cheat sheet resource guide, then just having a picture of the freebie — along with a widget where they can put in their name and email — will suffice.

If you're asking people to give you a serious investment in time — such as a webinar — then I'd think about perhaps having a quick video introducing yourself — and the webinar you're giving away.

Bonus Tip: Create a dedicated landing page that mentions "LinkedIn" somewhere — such as "Hey Fellow LinkedIn User! Feel free to grab my FREE Case Study!"

I know it seems trivial, but this small customized tweak can lower a prospect's resistance to your marketing message just enough to boost the conversion rate of your page by 10-15%.

LinkedIn Advertising Key #4: Determine WHO You Want to Target

This is where LinkedIn ads derive much of their

marketing power. (And the reason I so wholeheartedly recommend them for folks trying to reach specific occupations or businesses.)

Because with LinkedIn ads you can use the following criteria to target would-be leads:

- Job title
- Job function (sometimes even better than title)
- Industry
- Geography
- Company name
- Seniority
- Age
- Gender
- LinkedIn Group
- School
- Skill

There's virtually no limit to all the awesome — if super "Big Brother-y" — ways you can target LinkedIn users.

For instance, I've helped clients target "Male senior accountants over the age of 40 who went to Texas A&M University AND belong to the International Accounting LinkedIn Group…"

Or: "Oral surgeons over 50, who founded their own practice, have been in the industry over 25 years AND belong to the Oral and Maxillofacial LinkedIn Group." (Take that, Facebook!)

Now getting to this level of demographic sophistication will require you to know WHO the hell your ideal customer actually is.

For instance, one of my clients sold network security software. (At a high price.) And one would THINK that we wanted to target the "Head of IT" for "Fortune 500" companies.

Turns out, that was NOT our customer. In a corporate structure it's the CTO (Chief Technical Officer) who makes all the software decisions — not the "Head of IT." (Much to the chagrin of IT folks.)

Also, getting Fortune 500 companies to commit to software purchases is just slightly harder than understanding the federal tax code. (Most of these big companies are like "aircraft carriers" and getting them to commit to any decision is like herding cats.)

Instead, we needed to target CTOs of mid-sized companies. (But to discover that we needed to talk to get out of the ivory tower and talk to the sales guys and girls in the trenches.)

So, before you spend time — and hundreds of dollars in ad spend — take time conversing with your team (even if your team is just you and your Jack Russell Terrier) and figure out exactly who you want your ad to reach.

LinkedIn Advertising Key #5: Write Your Copy (Gather Your Creative)

So, the actual creative of your LinkedIn ad is very similar to the Google AdWords platform.

You must gather:

- A headline (That tells people who the ad is for)

- Some ad copy (Telling people what yer offering and what they need to do)
- Destination URL
- An image

Again, I am not the world's biggest LinkedIn expert. But here are a few things I've noticed having run a couple hundred of these types of ads:

- **Ask a question in your headline if you can.** The brain just responds differently to questions than it does commands. (Ask yourself which you would be more likely to click on "Reach New Customers" or "Wanna Reach New Customers?") And that "question mark" character also helps your headline stand out in a sea of other LinkedIn noise.

- **But…that doesn't mean your headline can be long.** You've only got 25 characters to play with, so make 'em count.

- **Get. To. The. Point.** (With your ad copy.) You don't have a lot of room here, so just start off with a verb telling people what you want them to do. ("Grab my FREE dental marketing cheat sheet & boost your business today!")

- **Put a female face in your image.** I know this might be a bit controversial. And objectifying. And not the most enlightened view of humanity. But all my testing has shown, putting a female face will boost click rates.

- **Resize your image to 50x50 pixels before uploading.** And make sure you can see what's going on in the image before publishing.

- **Add targeting to your destination URL.** Whether it's Google Analytics — or some other tracking — you definitely want to have some kind of tracking in place, so you can see how well — or not well — your ads are doing.

LinkedIn Advertising Key #6: Create That Ad (and Set Your Budget)

We've gone over most of this already, but all you do is:

- Head over to LinkedIn.com/Advertising and create a business account
- Upload your assets
- Set your daily budget (Remember start slow with $10/day and then raise from there)
- Set your CPC bid — I like to usually go $1-$2 over the minimum suggested bid (Don't worry — you won't be paying that)
- Create three different versions of your

ad — Try different tweaks (such as
different headlines, pictures, or ad copy)

- Allow people to have you "follow up"
  with them personally, as opposed to
  "clicking." (It's called lead collection,
  and it's awesome.)

- Let 'em rip (and by "rip" I mean go out
  there and make ya some money)

LinkedIn Advertising Key #7: Monitor (and Tweak)

I know this isn't exactly the sexiest part of marketing — constantly futzing with ads to make sure they're performing.

But it is where the REAL money is made.

That's because minor tweaks — or sometimes major tweaks — to your ad creative and targeting can make a huge difference down the line in terms of lead cost.

So, how do you know if your ad is successful?

Well, here are a couple of guidelines to keep in mind:

- **Give your ad at least three days** before freaking out…I mean…adjusting the ad.

- **A click-thru-rate of .025% or higher for a LinkedIn ad is a winner.** So, if you've got a particular ad variation that's reached that…you have your "control." (If not, keep trying out new variations.)

- **Once you've got a winner, create variations of the "control."** Not create "new" variations out of thin air. (Otherwise you won't know what works, and what doesn't.)

- **If your CTR is good** — but your opt-in rate or conversion rate is poor…your issue is that your offer isn't clear on your landing page. (Don't forget it's all about: Benefits! Benefits! Benefits!)

- **Break your ads into different campaigns, by company,**

> **occupation, title, etc**. When you can get this to work — you'll have hit upon the "hidden gold" of LinkedIn ads.
>
> - **Create "retargeting ads"** — using Facebook and/or Google — to follow those folks who don't opt-in. (Lets you get more profit out of the same amount of LinkedIn ad spend.)

And that's really what LinkedIn ads are all about. Wringing out more profit from every drop of LinkedIn ad spend. (Because when you can do that, the only question will be how I make even more money — by doing even less work.)

And that's what we will cover in the next chapter.

Chapter 7 Key Takeaways:

- *LinkedIn ads can be a fantastic way* to reach the most targeted professional audience anywhere. (Just be aware of the high CPCs.)

- *Be prepared to spend at least $100* in a LinkedIn Ad campaign. With a minimum daily bid of $10/day, this will give you plenty of time to test and tweak to find a winning ad.

- *There are TWO types of ads: display ads (text or video) or sponsored updates.* In my experience, display ads provide a bigger ROI.

- *Promote STUFF that puts folks into your funnel, first.* This usually means some kind of email opt-in or lead-collection. (Links to sales pages don't convert very well.)

- *The MAGIC of LinkedIn ads comes from its*

targeting. You can target based on things like Job Title, Job Function, Industry, Geography, Company Name, Age, Gender or LinkedIn Group.

- When writing ad copy try to put questions in your headlines — and keep your ad description focused on benefits.

- REAL ad success comes from finding a "control" — an ad that is currently working — and then tweaking that ad to make small, incremental improvements. (Doesn't sound earth shattering, but it will make a huge difference.)

Chapter 8:
Tools & Apps You Just Absolutely Gotta Have

"The best investment is in the tools of one's trade."
-Benjamin Franklin

Awesome! You have made it to my FAVORITE part of this tome.

Namely all the cool tools and apps that help you get a helluva lot done — and look like a total productivity wizard — even while you sit in your hammock setting your rotation for your Fantasy baseball team.

Now before we jump into my most indispensable LinkedIn marketing tools, I need to tackle one rather thorny and controversial topic…and that is third-party LinkedIn apps. (Or the obliteration of third-party apps.)

There was a magical time — back in the Paleozoic era of 2013 — when LinkedIn would let third-party companies, such as Amazon and WordPress, create applications that let you "decorate" your profile with things such as your:

- Amazon reading list
- Calendar
- Evernote

And you can STILL do a ton of cool ninja-app stuff with your LinkedIn profile. You gotta be sneakier about it. (Don't worry I'm gonna show you how.)

But I tell you this because MUCH of the information out there about LinkedIn apps is outdated and just plain wrong. (And I don't want you to waste your time looking for features that aren't there anymore.)

So, now I've got the official "safety cop" lecture out of the way, let's jump right in with my 4 Super-Killer, Must-Have LinkedIn Marketing Apps:

Must-Have LinkedIn App #1: IFTTT (If This, Then That)

If you're not familiar with IFTTT — and why would you be with such a weird name like that — prepare to have your mind blown.

IFTTT is a super-powerful app that lets you set up "rules" across any number of your digital footprints in the world. (And I mean ANY.)

For instance, you could set up rules that:

- You get an email each time a Silver-Age comic book is posted on Craigslist (or eBay)
- Your phone sends a text message to your kids when your near school to pick

them up

- Your refrigerator sends you an email when it's time to change the water filter (No joke)

- You receive an email when someone you follow on SoundCloud or Spotify uploads a new song (Or you can even receive a summary of all the songs you've liked that week)

- Your Fitbit exercise sessions — are automatically saved to a Google spreadsheet (In my case, this would be a short spreadsheet)

Now this all depends on your fridge or automobile having this technology in place. (Don't think my '83 Honda Civic could handle it.)

But these "recipes" — as they call them in the IFTTT parlance — can be super-powerful ways to stay productive, even while you sleep. (And this is especially true with our many social media properties.)

For instance we could set up "recipes" that:

- "If" we publish a new blog post — or YouTube video — "then" it's shared on our LinkedIn Profile
- "If" a link is posted on our Facebook page, "then" a copy is posted on LinkedIn
- "If" there's a popular article on the New York Times in my area of expertise, "then" it's shared with my LinkedIn followers
- "If" you broadcast on Periscope, "then" it's posted as an update on LinkedIn
- "If" it's Christmas (or someone's birthday), "then" that person receives a template message from us on LinkedIn

Now as you can see there literally thousands of ways to skin this LinkedIn cat. (And, trust me, you can spend hours looking through the many variations. I have.)

But, as a general rule, I would avoid having content you update many times throughout the day — such as Twitter or Instagram or a Foursquare check-in — automatically re-purposed on LinkedIn. (Fatigue will set in for your followers.)

But, for any pillar content — such as a blog post, video, or Facebook page update — I would definitely create some killer IFTTT recipes to help promote it. (Not to mention you might find that rare "Silver Surfer" comic book from the 70s you've been looking for.)

Must-Have LinkedIn App #2: Evernote (With IFTTT)

Evernote is another one of those life-changing apps I don't know how I survived without for so long. Although for years I thought the same thing about Netflix. ("You telling me I can watch episodes of "Columbo" AND "Rockford Files" ANYTIME I want!")

In case you're not familiar with this awesome tool — with the strange green elephant logo — Evernote is a FREE app — though you will need to pay $2.99/month for this feature I'm about to show you — that lets you store, gather and track almost everything you need in your life. (Articles, receipts, your boarding pass, that manifesto about the Arsenal football club you've been working on for 10 years.)

And what makes Evernote so powerful is that it syncs all this "content" across all your devices — both mobile and desktop. (And keeps all the formatting native to whatever you put in there.)

But the reason I LOVE Evernote so much — from a LinkedIn perspective — is its power to "scan" business cards on the spot and pull the contact info and send an instant LinkedIn connect invite. ("F&*in brilliant!")

This strategy gets even cooler when you pair it with IFTTT and set up a "recipe" that: "If I scan a business card with Evernote, then LinkedIn automatically sends that person an email of my choosing."

I can't emphasize enough how frickin' cool this is. How many times have you been at some conference and collected a crap load of business cards and then typed them into LinkedIn hoping they'll add you? (And then big whoop! So they add you! What next?)

Whereas, with this strategy, you can scan their card and if they "connect" with you, you'll have a customized email ready in place to capitalize on that new connect by:

- Providing them more information about your products and services
- Offering them a freebie
- Inviting them to check out testimonials about your product

Most people are so impressed with this little trick — especially if I show it to them in person — they assume I've got every other part of my business and life as sorted out. (How little they know!")

Now to set up this devilish piece of marketing Mojo you have to go through a couple of hoops. Luckily, I've created a little step-by-step process on my blog. You can access it over at PunkRockMarketing.com/EvernoteBizCard.

Must-Have LinkedIn App #3: HootSuite

So, HootSuite (the social media dashboard tool) isn't as earth-shattering as the first two. But it provides a valuable service: it lets you manage all your LinkedIn groups — and profile activity — in one tab. (Meaning you don't have to navigate around the LinkedIn universe to all the various groups — but instead can do everything from your smartphone or tablet.)

The tool is FREE — though they have paid options. (Haven't needed that yet.) And all you do is:

- Sign up for an account
- Download the app (If you like)

- Sync your HootSuite with your LinkedIn profile
- Create "streams" (these are Hootsuite's' versions of tabs) for each of your primary LinkedIn groups

And you don't have to just use HootSuite for LinkedIn. I use it primarily for my Twitter activities. (I don't recommend you use it for your Facebook page management. Facebook, in my experience, penalizes accounts that do their Fan Page publishing with a third-party app.)

But with the weekly LinkedIn Group interactions I recommend, primarily between Tuesday-Thursday, HootSuite is an absolute time-saver and stress-reducer. Not bad for something that costs you NOTHING.

Must-Have LinkedIn App #4: Social Lead Machine (Chrome App)

I've left this tool for last, because, frankly, it is

the most expensive ($40/month) and, if put into the wrong hands, can get your LinkedIn account banned quick.

But…if you've tried everything in this book, and you've got your LinkedIn profile and marketing funnel dialed in right where you want it, then I recommend you give this super-powerful tool a try.

Okay, so why's this tool so powerful?

The reason is simple: one of the easiest ways to get "noticed" by folks on LinkedIn — who are not already in your existing network — is to "view" their profile. (We're all vain and want to know who the heck checked out our profile.)

But this process can be laborious. (I mean, there's all those episodes of "Treehouse Masters" to get through.)

Unless you've got a piece of software such as Social Lead Machine. The process works something like this:

- You get your profile maximized for awesomeness (They've got some tutorials to help you with this)

- You determine who your ideal buyer or client is (You should already have a good idea if you've gone over the strategies outlined in this book)

- You search, using keywords, for LinkedIn users whose profile you'd like to visit.

- Let the software do its thing

I know what you're saying: sounds unbelievably spammy. You're right. It risks going into the dark arts of the LinkedIn Hogwarts School. (And there are many other products out there that cross the line.)

But having used a few of these products from the underbelly of the LinkedIn marketing world, I can tell you the guys over at Social Lead Machine go to great lengths to ensure the tool isn't used for nefarious means.

And in my experience, the BEST way to ensure that this strategy is effective (and ethical) is to ensure everything in your profile is inviting and relevant to folks you're viewing. (Not just something that sniffs of a sales-y fishing expedition.)

And I probably wouldn't recommend you try this powerful (though expensive) tool right out the LinkedIn marketing gate. But once you've got your funnel dialed in — and your profile primed for optimal lead-generation — this is a tool that can, within just a few weeks, provide a huge BOOST to your business. (Not to mention your ability to catch up on "Treehouse Masters.")

Chapter 8 Key Takeaways:

• **The author loves tools and apps because he's intrinsically lazy** — and likes to appear more productive and organized than he is.

• **The author has a slightly-uncomfortable man-crush on IFTTT (If Then, This That**). This app lets you create "recipes" or "rules" which will automate tasks. (Such as posting any new WordPress blog post or YouTube video or Periscope broadcast on your LinkedIn profile.)

• **Another great app — especially when used with IFTTT — is Evernote.** With these two tools you can "photo scan" somebody's business card, connect with them on LinkedIn, and send them an email touting your latest product or service — in less than five seconds.

- **HootSuite is a great way to manage all your social media activity — not just LinkedIn stuff.** The author uses it to monitor all his LinkedIn Groups, Twitter accounts, and Instagram activity.

- **Social Lead Machine ain't cheap, but it's one of the most powerful tools for automating your lead-generation** duties on LinkedIn. When you've got everything dialed in, give their 15-day FREE trial a chance.

Epilogue: Okay, What Next?

What next, indeed?

It's hard to know what the social media landscape — and that includes LinkedIn — is gonna require of us marketers over the next few years.

Is Facebook gonna take over the universe — and implant a microchip in our brain — to become the #1 search engine/media company/local business guide in the world…like most people think?

Maybe.

Will the Internet become a mish-mash of Pinterest pins and Tumblr .gifs and 60-second Instagram selfie videos? With anything longer than 250 words, or more substantive than a BuzzFeed article, left by the wayside. (''Five Reasons You Need to Read This Article (and #3 Will Shock You!)"

Maybe.

But I have a feeling no matter how visual and "click-bait-y" social media gets…

…there will always be a place for career-minded people who get up before 11 a.m. and would rather spend their weekends working on a marketing plan — than build a PVC pipe castle at "Burning Man."

And as LinkedIn rolls out more services and apps, the LinkedIn profile will be the default resume/portfolio/personal website. (Even more important than a company website.)

So the relationships you build on LinkedIn won't just help pad your earnings — which it will — but will put your company (and your career) in a prime strategic location for the future.

Where you won't be shocked by anything that comes your way. (Including "Reason #3 You Need to Read This Article."

And if you've enjoyed this book, or even if you didn't enjoy the book, would you be willing to leave a review?

Even a sentence or two really helps us indie authors carve out a career as a creative professional.

HEAD OVER to PunkRockMarketing.com/LIBook to leave a review on Amazon (and enjoy truckloads of good karma):

Oh, and just one more thing...

A Special FREE Gift for You!

If you'd like FREE instant access to my seminar "How to Make a Damn Good Living With Social Media (Even If You Hate Social Media" then head over to **PunkRockMarketing.com/Free**. (What else you gonna do? Watch another "Twilight" movie?!)

ALL RIGHTS RESERVED. No part of this publication may be reproduced or transmitted in any form whatsoever, electronic, or mechanical, including photocopying, recording, or by any informational storage or retrieval system without express written, dated and signed permission from the author.

DISCLAIMER AND/OR LEGAL NOTICES:

Every effort has been made to accurately represent this book and it's potential. Results vary with every individual, and your results may or may not be different from those depicted. No promises, guarantees or warranties, whether stated or implied, have been made that you will produce any specific result from this book. Your efforts are individual and unique, and may vary from those shown. Your success depends on your efforts, background and motivation.

The material in this publication is provided for educational and informational purposes only and is not intended as business advice. Use of the programs, advice, and information contained in this book is at the sole choice and risk of the reader.

Lightning Source UK Ltd.
Milton Keynes UK
UKHW022029250419
341619UK00005B/298/P

9 781970 119152